Ostriches

by Caroline Arnold
photographs by Richard R. Hewett

Lerner Publications Company • Minneapolis, Minnesota

To Gary and Wendy Teixiera
      —CA and RRH

The author and photographer would like to thank the Teixiera Ostrich Ranch, Maricopa, California; Wildlife Safari, Winston, Oregon; and the Los Angeles Zoo, Los Angeles, California.

Additional photographs courtesy of: Carolyn T. Arnold, p. 12; Patricia Ruben Miller/Independent Picture Service, p. 14 (right); Caroline S. Arnold, p. 31.

Thanks to our series consultant, Sharyn Fenwick, elementary science/math specialist. Mrs. Fenwick was the winner of the National Science Teachers Association 1991 Distinguished Teaching Award. She also was the recipient of the Presidential Award for Excellence in Math and Science Teaching, representing the state of Minnesota at the elementary level in 1992.

Early Bird Nature Books were conceptualized by Ruth Berman and designed by Steve Foley. Series editor is Joelle Riley.

Lerner Publications Company
A division of Lerner Publishing Group
241 First Avenue North
Minneapolis, MN 55401 U.S.A.

Website address: www.lernerbooks.com

Library of Congress Cataloging-in-Publication Data

Arnold, Caroline.
    Ostriches / by Caroline Arnold ; [photographs by Richard R. Hewett].
      p.   cm. — (Early bird nature books)
    Includes index.
    Summary: Describes the physical characteristics, behavior, and life cycle of the ostrich.
    ISBN 0-8225-3044-9 (lib. bdg.)
    1. Ostriches—Juvenile literature. [1. Ostriches.] I. Hewett, Richard R. II. Title. III. Series.
QL696.S9 A74 2001
598.5'24—dc21   99-045703

Manufactured in the United States of America
1 2 3 4 5 6 – JR – 06 05 04 03 02 01

Contents

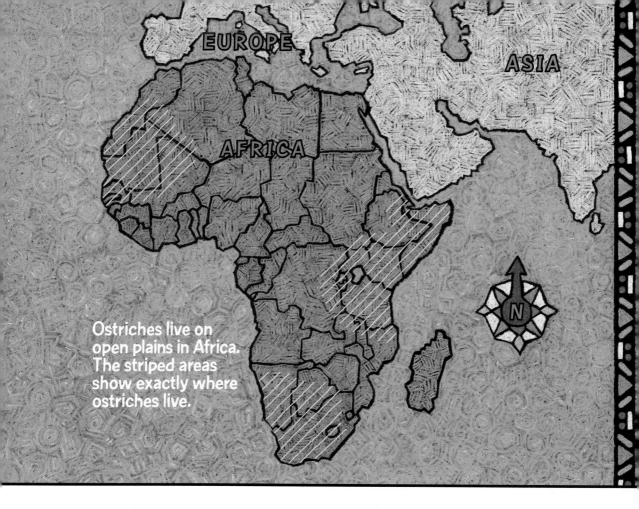

Ostriches live on open plains in Africa. The striped areas show exactly where ostriches live.

EUROPE

ASIA

AFRICA

N

Be a Word Detective

Can you find these words as you read about the ostrich's life? Be a detective and try to figure out what they mean. You can turn to the glossary on page 46 for help.

barb

herbivores

incubating

molting

precocial

predators

preens

quill

ratites

territory

Chapter 1

Ostriches live in Africa. How big are ostriches?

The Biggest Bird

Ostriches are the world's biggest birds. They have long legs, huge bodies, and skinny necks. Ostriches are taller than most other animals.

Adult ostriches are bigger than most people. They usually stand 6 to 8 feet tall. They weigh 200 to 300 pounds. But a very large ostrich may be 10 feet tall. Such a big ostrich weighs about 400 pounds.

The scientific name for the ostrich is Struthio camelus.

Male and female ostriches are about the same size. You can tell them apart by their coloring. Adult males are black and white. Adult females are brownish-gray.

The ostrich on the left is a female. The ostrich on the right is a male.

Young ostriches have brown, speckled feathers.

An ostrich's skin may be red, blue, or black. You can see the skin on an ostrich's legs. You can also see it along an ostrich's head and neck. Even though all ostriches do not look exactly alike, they are all the same species, or kind, of animal.

9

Ostriches have two toes on each foot (right). The bend in the middle of an ostrich's leg is not its knee. It is the ostrich's ankle (below).

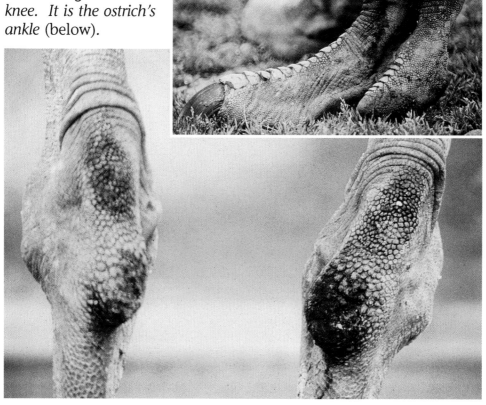

Most birds have three or more toes on each foot. Ostriches are unusual. They have only two toes. A sharp claw is at the end of each toe. The claws help the ostrich to grip the ground when it runs.

Ostriches walk on their toes. When an ostrich walks or runs, it looks as if its legs bend backward. That's because the bend we see in the middle of the leg is the ostrich's ankle.

An ostrich's knees are hidden under the feathers at the top of its legs.

Chapter 2

The long feathers on an ostrich's wings and tail are called plumes. How do feathers help an ostrich?

Fancy Feathers

Ostriches have long feathers on their wings and tails. Shorter feathers cover their bodies. Feathers protect an ostrich's skin. They help keep ostriches warm when nights are cool.

Ostriches do not have feathers on their legs or feet. Their legs and feet are protected by scales. Scales are small pieces of hard skin.

An ostrich has short, fluffy feathers on its body.

Each barb on an ostrich's feathers is separate. Most birds' feathers have barbs that are fastened to each other.

The stiff, center part of a bird's feather is called the quill. Each feathery strand along the quill is called a barb. Most birds have barbs that are fastened to each other. Each feather is smooth and flat. But an ostrich's barbs are all separate. That makes ostrich feathers soft and flowing.

An ostrich preens its feathers with its bill. Preening keeps the feathers clean and smooth. An ostrich's body makes a special oil. Preening spreads that oil over the feathers. This helps the ostrich stay dry when it rains. Water cannot soak into oily feathers.

The quills of an ostrich's feathers grow out of its skin.

An ostrich's bill acts like a comb. It straightens and cleans the ostrich's feathers. The bill also spreads body oil over the feathers.

Ostriches lose their feathers once a year. Then they grow new ones. This process is called molting. Just a few feathers fall out at a time. The ostrich always has some feathers to cover its body.

16

Chapter 3

*Two of these birds
are ostriches.
Where do most
birds live?*

Birds Who Cannot Fly

 Most birds are small animals. They live
in trees. And they can fly. Birds who fly have
light, hollow bones.

This bird is a cassowary. Cassowaries are ratites who live in Australia.

Ostriches have feathers and wings. But they are not like other birds. Ostriches belong to a group of birds called ratites (RAT-ites). Ratites have thick, heavy bones. Ostriches and other ratites live on the ground. They cannot fly. Instead, they run on sturdy legs.

Ostriches are herbivores (HUR-buh-vorz). Herbivores are animals who eat plants. Ostriches eat grass and small plants. Sometimes they eat insects and small animals, such as lizards and turtles.

When an ostrich eats, sometimes you can see lumps of food slide down its long neck.

Ostriches eat quickly. They snatch their food with their bills. Ostriches have no teeth. They cannot bite or chew. They swallow their food whole. While eating, ostriches also swallow sand and small pebbles. That helps to break the food into small pieces.

Ostriches use their bills to grab food.

Chapter 4

These ostriches are running across the flat African plain. Where do ostriches find food and water?

Ostrich Life

Ostriches live on the dry, open plains of Africa. Ostriches search for food and water in the grasslands. Sometimes water is scarce on the plains. Then ostriches stay in large groups near lakes and rivers.

Ostriches do not hide their heads in the ground. But sometimes it is hard to see an ostrich's head when it is eating grass.

Ostriches sometimes look like they are hiding their heads in the ground. Many people think ostriches put their heads in the ground when they are afraid. This is not true. Ostriches run away from danger.

These ostriches are watching for danger.

Ostriches are always on guard.

Ostriches can run 40 miles per hour. That's faster than a car driving along a city street. When an ostrich runs, it holds its wings out along its body. This may help the ostrich to keep its balance. It also helps it to turn quickly.

24

An ostrich can run for 20 minutes or more without stopping.

Cheetahs are the fastest animals who live on land. They sometimes leap on the backs of ostriches to kill them.

In Africa, large wildcats such as lions and cheetahs hunt ostriches. These animals are predators (PREH-duh-turz). Predators are animals who hunt and eat other animals. But ostriches have good eyesight. And they are always on the lookout for danger. Ostriches can usually spot their enemies. That way, ostriches can run away before a predator comes near.

Ostriches can also hear their predators.
Ostriches can hear well. An ostrich's ears are
small holes on each side of its head.

These ostriches are listening. Can you see their ears?

Chapter 5

Fights between ostriches can be noisy. What is the male ostrich on the left doing to the one on the right?

Family Life

Male ostriches are called roosters. Female ostriches are called hens. A family group usually has one rooster and several hens. A family lives in its own area. The area is called a territory. A male ostrich chases other roosters out of his territory.

All the hens in a family lay their eggs in one big nest. An ostrich's egg is about 8 inches long. It weighs 3 to 5 pounds. It is the biggest egg in the world.

Ostriches do not make nests like other birds. All the hens lay their eggs in one space on the ground.

Many parts of Africa have a rainy season and a dry season. Ostriches usually lay their eggs during the rainy season. Rain helps grass and other plants grow. So when the ostriches' eggs hatch, there will be plenty of food for all the birds to eat.

One ostrich egg is as big as two dozen chicken eggs.

The oldest hen usually sits on the nest during the day.
The rooster sits on the nest at night.

The rooster and the oldest hen take turns sitting on the eggs in the nest. Ostriches sit on their eggs to protect them. Sitting on the eggs also keeps them from becoming too hot or too cold. Sitting on eggs is called incubating (ING-kyoo-bait-ing) the eggs. Ostriches incubate their eggs for about six weeks. During that time a baby ostrich is growing inside each egg.

Hatching is hard work. Many hours go by as a baby ostrich breaks out of its shell.

A baby ostrich is called a chick. The chick peeps inside the shell when it is ready to hatch. It pecks against the inside of the shell. Finally it makes a tiny hole. The chick slowly makes the hole bigger until the shell cracks open.

Chapter 6

A newly hatched chick is about 12 inches tall. How long does the chick stay in its nest?

Growing Up

A newly hatched ostrich stays in the nest for two or three days. Then it is ready to go exploring.

These chicks are looking for food.

Chicks know how to walk as soon as they
hatch. They also know how to peck for food.
They do not need to be fed by their parents. Birds
who can feed themselves right after they hatch
are called precocial (prih-KOH-shuhl). Ostriches,
chickens, and ducks are all precocial birds.

All the hens in a family help to look after the young ostriches after they hatch. The chicks follow their family group across the plain. They must watch out for wild dogs, hyenas, eagles, and other predators.

Chicks huddle together for safety. They can run to hiding places together.

If danger is near, the adults in the family call out a loud warning. Then the chicks run to a hiding place or stand very still. Baby ostriches have speckled feathers. Speckled feathers are hard to see in tall grass. So predators cannot see chicks who are hiding in tall grass.

An adult ostrich warns its family with its booming voice.

These ostriches are six months old.

Young ostriches grow fast. For the first six months, they grow about 1 foot each month. By the time they are one year old, they are nearly adult size. Ostriches keep growing until they are four or five years old.

Young ostriches have gray and brown feathers. They grow their adult feathers when they are two or three years old. Then they leave their family groups. They begin families of their own.

Ostriches grow quickly. These ostriches are one year old.

Chapter 7

Ostriches have existed since long ago. How long do ostriches live?

Amazing Birds

Wild ostriches can live to be more than 40 years old. In zoos, some ostriches have lived much longer than that.

Ostriches are amazing. You can enjoy seeing these large flightless birds in zoos and wild animal parks. You can also see them on farms and ranches all over North America.

Ostriches are curious about everything.
This ostrich lives on a ranch.

Colored tags help people keep track of ostriches who are raised on ranches.

In many parts of the United States, people raise ostriches on farms and ranches in the same way that they raise chickens or cows. People raise ostriches for their feathers, meat, eggs, and skins.

42

In Africa, wild ostriches are protected. It is against the law to hunt them. As long as there are wild places for ostriches to live, these giant birds will continue to roam the African plains.

This female ostrich is walking in high grass. She holds her wings out for balance.

On Sharing a Book

As you know, adults greatly influence a child's attitude toward reading. When a child sees you read, or when you share a book with a child, you're sending a message that reading is important. Show the child that reading a book together is important to you. Find a comfortable, quiet place. Turn off the television and limit other distractions like telephone calls.

Be prepared to start slowly. Take turns reading parts of this book. Stop and talk about what you're reading. Talk about the photographs. You may find that much of the shared time is spent discussing just a few pages. This discussion time is valuable for both of you, so don't move through the book too quickly. If the child begins to lose interest, stop reading. Continue sharing the book at another time. When you do pick up the book again, be sure to revisit the parts you have already read. Most importantly, enjoy the book!

Be a Vocabulary Detective

You will find a word list on page 5. Words selected for this list are important to the understanding of the topic of this book. Encourage the child to be a word detective and search for the words as you read the book together. Talk about what the words mean and how they are used in the sentence. Do any of these words have more than one meaning? You will find these words defined in a glossary on page 46.

What about Questions?

Use questions to make sure the child understands the information in this book. Here are some suggestions:

What did this paragraph tell us? What does this picture show? What do you think we'll learn about next? Where do ostriches live? Could an ostrich live in your backyard? Why/Why not? What do ostriches eat? How does a chick break out of its shell? What do you think it's like being an ostrich? What is your favorite part of the book? Why?

If the child has questions, don't hesitate to respond with questions of your own such as: What do *you* think? Why? What is it that you don't know? If the child can't remember certain facts, turn to the index.

Introducing the Index

The index is an important learning tool. It helps readers get information quickly without searching throughout the whole book. Turn to the index on page 47. Choose an entry such as *feathers* and ask the child to use the index to find out how an ostrich's feathers help it stay dry. Repeat this exercise with as many entries as you like. Ask the child to point out the differences between an index and a glossary. (The index helps readers find information quickly, while the glossary tells readers what words mean.)

Where in the World?

Many plants and animals found in the Early Bird Nature Books series live in parts of the world other than the United States. Encourage the child to find the places mentioned in this book on a world map or globe. Take time to talk about climate, terrain, and how you might live in such places.

All the World in Metric!

Although our monetary system is in metric units (based on multiples of 10), the United States is one of the few countries in the world that does not use the metric system of measurement. Here are some conversion activities you and the child can do using a calculator:

WHEN YOU KNOW:	MULTIPLY BY:	TO FIND:
miles	1.609	kilometers
feet	0.3048	meters
inches	2.54	centimeters
gallons	3.787	liters
tons	0.907	metric tons
pounds	0.454	kilograms

Activities

Make up a story about ostriches. Be sure to include information from this book. Draw or paint pictures to illustrate your story.

Visit a zoo to see an ostrich. How are ostriches like other birds? How are they different? Is the ostrich molting? How can you tell?

Act out being an ostrich. How do you walk? What do you find to eat? How do you eat? How do you preen your feathers? What do you do when an enemy is near?

Glossary

barb—a soft strand along the side of an ostrich's feather

herbivores (HUR-buh-vorz)—animals who eat plants

incubating (ING-kyoo-bait-ing)—sitting on eggs to keep them at the right temperature so they will hatch

molting—losing feathers so new ones can grow in

precocial (prih-KOH-shuhl)—knowing how to walk and find food at the time of hatching

predators (PREH-duh-turz)—animals who hunt and eat other animals

preens—cleans and smooths feathers

quill—the stiff center of a bird's feather

ratites (RAT-ites)—large birds with thick, heavy bones

territory—an area where a family of ostriches lives

Index

Pages listed in **bold** type refer to photographs.

About the Author

Caroline Arnold is the author of more than 100 books for young readers. Her well-received Lerner Publishing Group titles include *Bobcats, Cats, Cats: In from the Wild, Saving the Peregrine Falcon, A Walk on the Great Barrier Reef,* and *Watching Desert Wildlife.* She grew up in Minneapolis, Minnesota, and studied art at Grinnell College and the University of Iowa. Ms. Arnold lives in Los Angeles, California.

About the Photographer

Richard R. Hewett was born and raised in St. Paul, Minnesota. He graduated from California's Art Center School of Design with a major in photojournalism. He has illustrated more than 50 children's books and collaborated with Caroline Arnold on the Lerner Publishing Group titles *Bobcats, Cats, Saving the Peregrine Falcon, Tule Elk,* and *Ostriches and Other Flightless Birds.* Dick and his wife, writer Joan Hewett, live in southern California.

The Early Bird Nature Books Series

African Elephants	Manatees	Scorpions
Alligators	Moose	Sea Lions
Ants	Mountain Goats	Sea Turtles
Apple Trees	Mountain Gorillas	Slugs
Bobcats	Ostriches	Swans
Brown Bears	Peacocks	Tarantulas
Cats	Penguins	Tigers
Cougars	Polar Bears	Venus Flytraps
Crayfish	Popcorn Plants	Vultures
Dandelions	Prairie Dogs	Walruses
Dolphins	Rats	Whales
Giant Sequoia Trees	Red-Eyed Tree Frogs	Wild Turkeys
Herons	Saguaro Cactus	Zebras
Jellyfish	Sandhill Cranes	